better together*

*This book is best read together, grownup and kid.

a kids book about™ optimism!

by Meir Kay

a
kids
book
about™

Printed in the United States of America

Library of Congress cataloging available.

A Kids Book About books are exclusively available online
on the A Kids Book About website.

To share your stories, ask questions, or inquire about bulk
purchases (schools, libraries, and nonprofits), please use
the following email address:

hello@akidsbookabout.com

www.akidsbookabout.com

ISBN: 978-1-951253-42-4

This book is dedicated to my parents
for their love, support, and fitting
me with the right pair of glasses.

Intro

Life is full of choices. What to eat for breakfast, what color to paint the new patio, or what to wear to your new job interview.

Some of our choices have a larger impact on our lives, like who we vote for, purchasing a house, and where to send the kids to school. But then there are the choices that define our lives, one of which is how we choose to view the world and the events that happen to us.

Being optimistic is a choice that we all have the power to make every day. I've dedicated my life to spreading this message and I'm optimistic that within these pages your kid and the kid in your heart will learn what optimism is truly about and how to make the choice to live this way today.

Hello,

my name is Meir and it is my privilege to share my thoughts on beard growth and its connection to climate change, flannel shirts, and how to utilize it for storing your lunch for a later time.

(see figure A1.0)

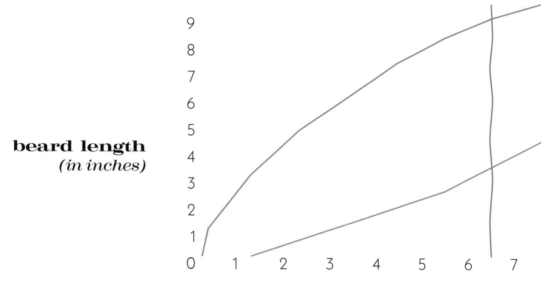

super-official graph:
figure A1.0

beard length
(in inches)

how much flannel *(# of shirts)*
food saved *(in ounces)*
the climate *(not really sure)*

Not what you expected?

How are you feeling about reading
the rest of this book?

Excited? Bored? Disappointed?
Or ready to stop reading and
go make a sandwich?

*Well, I guess you'll have to turn the page
to see what's next.*

HIGH

FIVE!

You turned the page!!

do it again!

This

is actually a book about optimism. But my name is really Meir*.

*pronounced "Mayor"

And believe it or not,
I really am excited to
tell you about optimism.

Optimism can be a hard word to say.
I like to say

Up-To-Me——

—ism

because it's *up to me* to be optimistic.
It's totally quite definitely, for sure,
entirely, 100000% up to me.

I use optimism every day.

Optimism is like **glasses** I wear
to change how I see the world.

Optimism is the **fuel** I use to follow my
dreams and live every day to the fullest.

Optimism is the **song** I choose
to dance to on the dance floor of life.

Even on the darkest days, I can still
find a way to see the good around me.

But Meir, what *is* optimism?

I'm glad you asked!

Let me tell ya.

Optimism

[op-*tuh*-miz-*uh*m**]**

is a choice you make every day to be cheerful, confident, and curious about life.

*super-official definition from the extra-smart and definitely official World Dictionary of Meir.

Sometimes people think optimism means....

...being

happy all the time,

not feeling any negative emotions,

nothing should ever get you down,

or just not thinking too much about things so that you'll be happy.

I'm here to tell you it doesn't mean any of those things.

It's so much

more.

Optimism

is first and foremost a choice.
I can **choose** to see a problem
as an opportunity or
chance to grow.

That's an

Up-To-Me

way of thinking.

You aren't born
an *optimist**
or a *pessimist**,
you choose either.

Optimist

[**op**-*tuh*-mist]

means someone who has optimism.

Pessimist

[pes-*tuh*-mist]

means someone who doesn't have optimism.

again from the super-official, extra-smart, and definitely real World Dictionary of Meir.

One

time while playing on the playground
I fell and broke my right arm.

It hurt and I was sad about it,
but after the doctor put on my cast—
I had a choice to make.

Continue to be sad and blame myself, be afraid that my classmates would make fun of me, and complain about the things I couldn't do with a cast.

Accept that it was an accident, I made a mistake, my friends would get to decorate my cast, my arm would get better eventually, and I'll have an awesome story to tell.

Another

time, I moved to a new school, leaving a place that I knew and many friends behind— again I had a choice to make.

I could have focused on what I would be missing, be sad about it, and look at the future with fear.

I could decide to put on my optimistic glasses and see it as a chance to make new friends and discover a new place.

Can

you tell the difference
between the two choices?

One embraces **fear** and the

other embraces **optimism.**

Optimism

is something you get better at
with practice.

Like your *handwriting*
or **cool dance moves**—
you didn't start out being awesome!

You don't start out good at optimism either,
and it's OK to not be perfect at it.

Optimism

is about living in the now,
being present today.

No one knows what will
happen in the future.

But you can know what will happen
right now by doing it.

By choosing it.

Optimism can still be there even when things are not great.

We all know that hard and messy things happen, but they are not the *only* things that happen.

When messy things happen,
it's like sitting in a dark room.

You can't see anything.

optimism

is the light switch—
it helps you to see MORE.

Like the things that bring you
joy, comfort, and possibility.

optimism

sees the opportunities, not the problems.

You can look at what might go wrong,
or at everything that could go right...

Think good and

it
will
be
good.

Optimism sounds pretty great, huh?

But it wasn't always easy for me.
It took a lot of practice, and
I still don't always get it right.

But that's OK.

I'm still learning, and I want to help you learn too.

So let's do this!

Here are my 6 tools for living out optimism every day...

1 Choose to see what's good **first.**

Instead of only focusing on the hard things, take a look at some of the good things.

2

Use the **language**
of optimism.

Don't say words like
bad or wrong, instead
say not good or not right.

3 Spend time with **optimistic people.**

Invite friends into your life who
uplift you and bring you joy.

4 Plan for tomorrow, just don't **worry** about it.

Don't ruin today by focusing on things
you can't control tomorrow.

5 Go easy on yourself.

Give yourself permission
to try and make mistakes.

You're learning.

6 Let go of your **expectations.**

Take things for what they are,
not what you expect them to be.

Now

you've got some tools to
practice optimism every day*.

*high-five the person reading this book with you!

And guess what happens when you do?

om!

*Benefits!

Friends want to hangout with you more because you're so positive.
Like laughing, optimism is contagious.

You've got more gratitude
for even the little things.
Can you name 3 things now?

You feel less stressed out and pressured.
Aren't you feeling better already?

Your sense of humor is off the charts.
Why did the chicken cross the road?*

*he was feeling optimistic!

Did I mention you're more:
happy
cheerful
confident
creative and
just overall awesome
when you practice optimism?

Not only
are you open to new possibilities,
but more show up all the time.

Then somehow, the world
becomes full of opportunities.

Full of
magic.

Because **optimism** shines a light even when there's darkness.

And not just for you,
but for others around you.

So choose optimism
today and every day.

Outro

igh-five!

You made it to the end of this book and the beginning of a new way to view the world!

So what's next?

Like any new skill, it takes practice, so remind your kid to be gentle with themselves and that each day brings a new opportunity to practice optimism. Check in with yourself and with your kid at the end of the day and see where they were optimistic or how they could sprinkle more optimism in their lives.

So flip on the optimism switch and start seeing the world in a whole new light.

find more kids books about

emotions, gratitude, change, bullying, death, empathy, anxiety, racism, failure, voting, and god.

akidsbookabout.com

share your read*

*Tell somebody, post a photo, or give this book away to share what you care about.

@akidsbookabout